Edna O'Brien

THE IRISH WRITERS SERIES
James F. Carens, General Editor

TITLE	*AUTHOR*
SEAN O'CASEY	Bernard Benstock
J. C. MANGAN	James Kilroy
W. R. RODGERS	Darcy O'Brien
STANDISH O'GRADY	Phillip L. Marcus
PAUL VINCENT CARROLL	Paul A. Doyle
SEUMAS O'KELLY	George Brandon Saul
SHERIDAN LEFANU	Michael Begnal
AUSTIN CLARKE	John Jordan
BRIAN FRIEL	D. E. S. Maxwell
DANIEL CORKERY	George Brandon Saul
EIMAR O'DUFFY	Robert Hogan
MERVYN WALL	Robert Hogan
FRANK O'CONNOR	James Matthews
JOHN BUTLER YEATS	Douglas Archibald
LORD EDWARD DUNSANY	Zack Bowen
MARIA EDGEWORTH	James Newcomer
MARY LAVIN	Zack Bowen
OSCAR WILDE	Edward Partridge
SOMERVILLE AND ROSS	John Cronin
SUSAN L. MITCHELL	Richard M. Kain
J. M. SYNGE	Robin Skelton
KATHARINE TYNAN	Marilyn Gaddis Rose
LIAM O'FLAHERTY	James O'Brien
IRIS MURDOCH	Donna Gerstenberger
JAMES STEPHENS	Brigit Bramsback
BENEDICT KIELY	Daniel Casey
EDWARD MARTYN	Robert Christopher
DOUGLAS HYDE	Gareth Dunleavy

EDNA O'BRIEN

Grace Eckley

Lewisburg

BUCKNELL UNIVERSITY PRESS

Associated University Presses, Inc.
Cranbury, New Jersey 08512

Library of Congress Cataloging in Publication Data

Eckley, Grace.
    Edna O'Brien.

    (The Irish writers series)
    Bibliography: p.
    1. O'Brien, Edna.
PR6065.B7Z65   823'.9'14   79–168806
ISBN 0–8387–7838–0.
ISBN 0–8387–7976–X (pbk.)

Contents

Introduction

Edna O'Brien's talent was early recognized for its natural lyrical qualities; according to the *New Statesman* (July 16, 1960), "She does not appear to have to strive to establish anything [in *The Country Girls*]; the novel, one feels, is so completely, so truly realised in the writer's mind that everything that comes out has a quality of life which no artifice could achieve." The quality of insight, also, is sustained throughout her works. In *The New Yorker* (February 12, 1972) Pauline Kael wrote, "Reading Edna O'Brien's fiction, I've been surprised by perceptions of what I thought no one else knew—and I wasn't telling." Yet Miss Kael expressed disappointment that Miss O'Brien "didn't move outside the magic circle of women's emotional problems." Approaching this subject almost obliquely, Peter Wolfe (*Saturday Review,* February 17, 1968) questioned the reader's involvement in *Girls in Their Married Bliss,* in which the characters are not interested in "music, sports, or handicrafts" and are little affected by "family, religion, and politics." He asked, "Do social institutions and ties matter as little as Miss O'Brien suggests? Are we so desperately detached from any living tradition or ideas?"

At the heart of the matter of reader response is what
Marcel Proust implied in the observation that "In reality,
each reader reads only what is already within himself."
Confronted with the question "What makes good, or
great, literature?" few would agree that the human heart
stripped of public supports makes even acceptable literature. Yet Miss O'Brien's women unhesitantly acknowledge
sexual necessity while living independently of public
concerns; her feminists rarely recognize that their cause
is public. Instead their object is love, and their sorrow is
its loss. The mother of "the lonely girl" dies, and mother-
lessness continues through the trilogy and into *Night;*
in *August Is a Wicked Month* a woman's only son
dies and the novel is filled with death images; in
Casualties of Peace the woman herself is accidentally
murdered just when she and a dark lover have found
happiness. The fear of loss is an ever-present burden of
living; moreover, it is a dominant attribute of love. In
an interview for *Talking to Women,* Edna O'Brien said
to Nell Dunn, "There's a beautiful poem of Yeats's which
I think is the meaning of love. 'It is a pity beyond all
telling, is hid in the heart of love. The folks who are buying
and selling, the clouds on their journey above. These and
the cold wet wind threaten the one that I love.' And that
marvellous solicitude, you know, that your loved one is
in danger. I have this for my children. If it's raining
and they're not with me I think they're out in the rain and
I suppose that's love."

Still a second factor exposed by Miss O'Brien's literary
stethoscope should cause more discomfort than this
exclusive submergence in the love theme, and that is the
thoroughness with which one's choice of someone to

love defines the entire range of one's personality; it exposes a streak of masochism, describes one's pathetic ideals, or reflects conditions of loneliness. "In a marriage or in an intimate relationship," Miss O'Brien remarked of *Casualties of Peace*, "I think the cruelty of the one party is willed or wished or maybe even egged on by the need for the cruelty in the other party." When Kate's divorce lawyer in *Girls* inquires, "What did you marry a man like that for?" she replies lamely, "It seemed to be what I wanted." The young woman of "How to Grow a Wisteria," looking back on a disrupted marriage with a "man who insisted on exile," realizes the changed attitudes that experience brings: "his disposition and his face fitted in with some brainless dream of hers."

For several kinds of love, *The Country Girls* offers the widest range of possibilities at the same time that it reveals the transience of any single love or interpretation of another's love. First is Caithleen's love of the hired man, Hickey, an extension of preadolescent fondness. But preadolescent certainty soon stretches into adolescent ambiguity: Hickey has green teeth, washes scantily if at all in the rainbarrel, and urinates nightly in a peach-tin, which he empties out the bedroom window to the detriment of shrubs and white flag. More important is the love of the mother, expressed with confidence by the small child in the declaration, "I was everything in the world to her, everything." Part of Edna O'Brien's continued search for romantic love, however, also appears in the depiction of the mother, who has apparently never totally surrendered her dream of romantic happiness. The mother's pathetic desire to be loved by a man who deserved her respect leads to a watery grave with her lover. Those who love these people, consequently, are deprived of the funeral ceremony, their last expression of love. Motherless, the child knows unexpected love from the teenage Molly, an underprivileged scullery maid in the Brennan household. The veterinarian, Mr. Brennan, who invites Caithleen to live with his family, reveals real tenderness for her and defends her against the drunken rampages and physical abuse of her father. Another love is that of Mr. Gentleman, an elderly friend who confines his lovemaking to kisses. His failure to keep an appointment with Caithleen at the end of the novel occurs because of commitments to others— his ailing wife and Caithleen's father—in the name of love; and those two relationships only emphasize the empty formalities of spoken affection as opposed to the rarity of actual feeling.

Through observing Edna O'Brien's handling of many kinds of love one may approach an answer to Peter Wolfe's third, difficult, yet pertinent question: "Conceding the difficulty of summoning moral principles in times of stress, do these stresses always take a sexual form?" Almost in answer, Miss O'Brien said at Durham, "I am interested in the love of children and the love of old people and the love of life and the impossibility and the possibility of love and the love of God, or the idea of God. And just the sense of love. Of the blessing of life really, of being able to be alive and be in touch with people's minds and with people's development and with people's magnitude." In the final analysis, loneliness and independence must be acknowledged as dominant themes in Edna O'Brien's fiction. Stresses, especially those of loneliness, most dramatically take the form of a quest for someone to love, and that person not only has a body but also re-flects the protagonist's state of mind.

A third aspect of meeting (or finding) ourselves can also cause discomfort, and this occurs in Edna O'Brien's works because of what has been called her "barnyard ro-bustness." Stethoscope becomes fluoroscope and exposes those elements which many people prefer to thrust into their buried minds. In *Girls,* for example, Miss O'Brien writes, "Kate [in a used furniture shop] felt disgust. A smell of homes that were, stained mattresses, mildewed, bed ends on which hands had laid the pickings from their noses; sofas farted into, the dregs of lives."

But the love theme thus far has dominated critical reaction, and although only three of Miss O'Brien's published books are Irish (*The Country Girls, The Lonely Girl, A Pagan Place*), she is famous in her own country for having written banned books; readers who know this make what Sean McMahon of *Eire-Ireland* (Spring, 1967) calls "an unfair mental equation: Edna O'Brien = Sex." Benedict Kiely, writing in *Conor Cruise O'Brien Introduces Ireland,* admits that she has been "brutally direct" and that "those moles the censors, or whoever eggs them on to their idiocies, are not able to take it." The pathological quality of the adverse criti-cism (to which Kiely calls our attention) is apparent in that by Bruce Arnold of *The Irish Times* (November 21, 1966):

Edna O'Brien's concern has been with the presentation of sex as a mixture of the furtive, the absurd, the inconsequential and the humorous adjunct to human endeavor. It has rarely been a question of passion. It has been exhibitionistic. It has dealt with, or hinted at, sacrilegious sex, lesbianism, venereal disease, voyeurism, fetishism, and various other forms of sexual frustration. Her novels in this respect deal almost exclusively with sexual failure.

Yet sexual failure, where it occurs in Edna O'Brien's works, is often the result of choice and of religious background and is countered by a staunch independence that all Miss O'Brien's heroines, though some are unaware of it, exhibit (Mary Hooligan of *Night* turns an array of sexual, and other, reminiscences into triumphant humor and rebounds from her last disappointment with admirable courage to face the future). Of the reader's retention of sexual stresses as the dominant impression of her books, Edna O'Brien remarked, as reported by Sean McMahon, "in a story of 70,000 words 3000 at most might deal directly with sex; 'if these 3000 are pored over to the virtual exclusion of the other 67,000 whose fault is that?'"

Miss O'Brien's novels—written for the most part in the first person—give the impression that they are a personal odyssey beginning with the background in County Clare, the convent school education, removal to London, birth of children, and dissolution of marriage. Several critics accurately sensed a deep personal wound that provokes revenge against men through the diabolical male characters—Herod, Eugene Gaillard, Dr Flaggler— and should have recognized Ernest Gebler's initials in the name Eugene Gaillard. But other dominant plot lines are not autobiographical; for example, although in several of her novels and short stories, the heroine's mother is dead, Miss O'Brien's mother is still living. Moreover, she seldom makes a writer one of her characters, although her personal successes in this area—which do not appear in her fiction—include many television plays (omitted from this analysis because of their fleeting form).

More important than biographical details that may provide mere frameworks for fiction are Miss O'Brien's personal convictions derived from the perceptions that color her world and form her concept of truth. For this reason I have quoted from interviews, including my own visits with her on January 4 and 5, 1972; and these, except my own, are acknowledged in the text.

In recent years Miss O'Brien's adherence to her concept of truth and her persistent exposure of factors which many persons would prefer not to think about has, among some critics, won her favor and admiration for her honesty and courage. Where Mary Hooligan's soliloquy resembles that of Molly Bloom, Anatole Broyard of *The New York Times* (December 28, 1972), in reviewing *Night*, wrote that "Mary's soliloquy is at once more savage and more tender than Molly's. The younger woman ends on 'Yes I said yes I will Yes,' but Mary has used up most of her yesses. Still, she will not surrender to 'no.'" Edna O'Brien does not quarrel with the masculine viewpoint as expressed in Joyce's *Ulysses* but describes much independence of it. Mary Hooligan at the close of *Night* faces her future without Molly's securities of house and husband and husband's income. Mary will not cavil, and she will endure.

Chronology

1930   Born December 15 in Tuamgraney, County Clare, Ireland, of Michael O'Brien and Lena, née Cleary. One brother, John, and two sisters, Patsy and Eileen.

1936   Began attending National School, Scarriff, County Clare.

1941   Enrolled in Convent of Mercy, Loughrea, County Galway.

1946   Entered Pharmaceutical College of Ireland, Dublin.

1948   Began contributions to the *Irish Press*.

1951   Married Ernest Gebler (marriage dissolved, 1964).

1952   Son, Carlos, born.

1954   Son, Sasha, born.

1959   Moved to London. Wrote *The Country Girls* in the first month of residence.

1960   *The Country Girls* published by Hutchinson, London, and by Alfred A. Knopf, New York.

1962   *The Lonely Girl* published by Jonathan Cape, London, and Random House, New York.

A Cheap Bunch of Nice Flowers staged at New Arts Theatre, London, premiere November 20, 1962.

1963   *A Cheap Bunch of Nice Flowers* in *Plays of the Year*, 26, ed. J. C. Trewin, published by Frederick Ungar, New York.

1964   *Girls in Their Married Bliss* published by Jonathan Cape, London.

Girl with Green Eyes, screenplay, adapted from the novel *The Lonely Girl*.

Girl with Green Eyes, a reprint of *The Lonely Girl*, published by Penguin Books, London.

1965   *August Is a Wicked Month* published by Jonathan Cape, London, and by Simon and Schuster, New York.

1966   *Casualties of Peace* published by Jonathan Cape, London.

Time Lost and Time Remembered, screenplay, written with Desmond Davis from the short story "A Woman at the Seaside" by Miss O'Brien.

1967   *Casualties of Peace* published by Simon and Schuster, New York.

1968   *The Love Object*, a short story collection, published by Jonathan Cape, London.

Girls in Their Married Bliss published by Simon and Schuster, New York.

Three Into Two Won't Go, screenplay, adapted from the novel by Andrea Newman.

1969   *The Love Object* published by Alfred A. Knopf, New York.

1970   *A Pagan Place* published by Alfred A. Knopf, New York. Received *Yorkshire Post* Award for Novel of the Year (*A Pagan Place*).

1971   *Zee & Co*, screenplay, published by Weidenfeld and Nicholson, London.

1972   *X, Y and Zee*, screenplay, produced.

A Pagan Place, stageplay, adapted from the novel, premiere November 2, 1972 at Royal Court Theatre, London.

Night published by Weidenfeld and Nicholson, London.

Edna O'Brien

The Personal Odyssey

Edna O'Brien, writer of nine books, four successful screenplays, and additional television plays, stage plays, and short stories, has just turned forty; and in twelve years of publication, she has experienced a bad press in her native Ireland for a number of critical reasons: she writes about sex; she is a woman; worse, she is a feminist; she is a well-known personality; and her theme is love.

Irish writers have long battled for literary freedom in their own country; in "The Whores on the Half-Doors or An Image of the Irish Writers" Benedict Kiely recognizes that Edna O'Brien's position as a woman writer is particularly sensitive:

The current determined persecution of the novels of Edna O'Brien is a case that calls for particular study. Is it caused by a hangover (the Irish time lag) from days before women got the vote, from a feeling that while it's bad and very bad for a man to speak out and tell the truth it is utterly unthinkable that a woman (bringing shame on the fair daughters of Erin) should claim any such liberty, especially a woman who had been educated, as the saying goes, at one of the best convent schools.

Basic to the criticism by the Irish of Irish writers is, of course, the fear of an unfavorable presentation. Answering such criticism, Edna O'Brien said in 1971, "I have only written three novels about Ireland . . . and you people seem to be oversensitive about it. . . . I am not writing for the Tourist Board! Nobody outside this country considers that I write a condemnation of Irish life; they just take it that I am writing about a set of people in Ireland" (*Hibernia,* December 3, 1971). That picture-postcard distortion cannot be expected from her, Miss O'Brien had indicated more than once. In the University of Durham interview, she said, "what makes a novel, or any work of art valid, is the degree of truth and authenticity behind it." And her goal is, always, to write a "truer book."

While Kiely has faith in the "convent girl with her temper riz" to break through some of the shackles on the Irish intellect, Edna O'Brien in person seems an unlikely candidate for contention and dissension. *Publishers Weekly* (May 25, 1970) described her accurately as a "smashing red-haired Irish beauty." In a melodious, dramatic voice, Miss O'Brien answers questions sincerely and directly; she seems not to fear being misunderstood or misquoted. With a quality of living the characters she creates, she gives the impression she might well have chosen a stage career except for a life-long ambition to write. "I believe I wrote, in my head, before I talked," she said. "I am told by my parents and by the people I knew in my childhood that I always wrote. And that on my way home from school I used to sit down in certain places, again secret places, and just write something in my little copybook. I used to have copybooks for what I called make-up people. So I gather that I always wrote. I think that the hunger, the quest to write, was always with me" (Durham interview).

The rural place of her childhood was County Clare in the West of Ireland, of which she said "Clare is an enchanting and enchanted place. I'm interested in the bones and stones of a place" (*Publishers Weekly*). The home village of Scarriff, which may be discerned with its "five street lamps" in such stories as "Irish Revel," prompted an interest in literature through three books, *Gone with the Wind, Rebecca,* and *How Green Was My Valley,* which, Miss O'Brien told *Publishers Weekly,* were "so precious that they were handed around from house to house in separate pages." The town provided a National School education where a local teacher encouraged Miss O'Brien's love of writing until the age of twelve when she journeyed to Loughrea east of Scarriff in County Galway to spend four years in the Convent of Mercy there. The convent school background is best described in *The Country Girls* and in the short story "Sister Imelda."

The next four years, spent in the Pharmaceutical College of Ireland in Dublin (1946–50) are not, thus far, fictionalized in her work, except perhaps at the end of *August* in the incident of Ellen's obtaining medicines for a venereal infection. The fictional Caithleen (Kate) and her namesakes work mainly in grocer's, rather than chemist's shops. Other experiences were more important, primarily that the first book Miss O'Brien bought in Dublin was one by James Joyce. "Reading bits of Joyce," she said, "was the first time in my whole life that I happened on something in a book that was exactly like my own life. I had always been a stranger from what had been my life up to then" (*Publishers Weekly*). In 1948 Miss O'Brien began writing "descriptive bits" for the Irish papers, and, reports *Publishers Weekly,* "She was encouraged in her writing by Paedar O'Donnell of the now defunct Dublin magazine, *The Bell,* who helped many an Irish writer on his way."

In 1951 Miss O'Brien married Ernest Gebler, who is also a writer of three novels; two sons, Carlos and Sasha, were born, in 1952 and 1954, and no doubt account for much of the beauty, delicacy, humor, and honesty of her presentation of children and her especially skillful handling of their dialogue. "The most honest relationship I've had with anyone has been with my children," she said. In private life she sees the protection of "the young and the floating" as an especial moral obligation. As she said to Nell Dunn, "I'm really only interested in protecting the ignorant or the young, or the stupid, or the unknowing." This special regard for "the young and the floating" accounts for much of the success of Miss O'Brien's first two novels.

When the family moved to London in 1959, Edna O'Brien wrote her first novel (not her first *attempt* at a novel) in the first three weeks. "I realise now that I would have had to leave Ireland in order to write about it. Because one needs the formality and the perspective that distance gives in order to write calmly about a place. Ireland is a wonderful incubator and . . . I would rather be from Ireland or Russia as a writer than from any other country. To live there and actually write is quite difficult; it's not simply the question of censorship" (Durham interview). Of the fluent writing of *Country Girls* (1960), she said, "it wrote itself; my arm held the pen."

The first novel, now published in twelve languages other than English, traces the tender development of Caithleen Brady from age fourteen, when her beloved mother dies in a boating accident, to age seventeen when, freed from a convent through a ruse devised by her friend Baba, Caithleen finds employment in Dublin. There an expected rendezvous with Mr. Gentleman fails to materialize and she is left in a very ordinary Dublin, with neither glamor nor hope.

In 1962 Miss O'Brien published *The Lonely Girl* as a sequel to *The Country Girls* and again won critical acclaim. In this second novel, Caithleen Brady is now twenty-one and has been employed in a Dublin grocery store for two years. She develops an attraction toward an older man, Eugene Gaillard, and stays with him at his house in Wicklow. Once her incensed father abducts her and another time he attempts a raid to rescue her from Eugene. At the same time she is pulled in an opposite direction from "respectability" by the sophisticated Eugene's scorn for her "Stone Age ignorance and religious slavery." Extremely sensitive and self-critical, she gropes a painful way toward self-development, finally by flight to England. (Miss O'Brien rewrote this novel as a very successful screenplay *Girl With Green Eyes,* and the original novel was republished by Penguin in 1964 under the film title.)

Living in England not only established the necessary distance for writing about Ireland but also provided new background and important connections. After *The Lonely*

Girl, Edna O'Brien turned to writing another kind of novel—the urbane—the kind that the folks back home deplored but that *Publishers Weekly* called an "escape from the rigid parochialism of Irish Catholicism and Irish country ways." How did she do it? they asked. "I think I have a great hunger and curiosity for life and growth," she said. "I have been very lucky in that I have had wonderful access to people who have brought me on." The trend was inevitable, both for author and characters; but perhaps because a great part of the fiction of childhood is a willing delusion, the audience who applauded the innocence of *The Country Girls* failed to observe the relationship between Caithleen's parents, which acts as a forewarning that the child who is loved by many people will not be loved for the same reasons when her body matures or her mind develops.

Consequently, this third novel, *Girls in Their Married Bliss,* with its bitter and ironic title, does not sustain the common "happily ever after" fiction and instead reflects disappointment, upheaval, and the dissolution of marriage. Caithleen's innocence, already dissolving at the end of *The Lonely Girl,* disappears proportionately as she discovers the savagery of her husband. That savagery is counterposed by her own weaknesses, which he no longer thinks are charming. Baba becomes pregnant by a lover and plays her husband's sexual impotence against his male ego and his desire to avoid scandal to extort from him both financial support and acknowledged fatherhood. Baba has no compassion for her husband about this extortion because she knows men well. "There isn't a man alive wouldn't kill any woman the minute she draws attention to his defects," she remarks. Certainly a growing awareness of what it means to be woman emerges mainly in the statements of Baba and gives Miss O'Brien a "feminist" label. Seeing women mistreated by both doctors and husbands, Baba, as she lies with feet in stirrups while being prodded by a gynecologist, protests, "Oh God, who does not exist, you hate women, otherwise you'd have made them different. And Jesus, who snubbed your mother, you hate them more. Roaming around all that time with a bunch of men, fishing; and sermons-on-the-mount. Abandoning women. I thought of all the women who had it, and didn't even know when the big moment was, and others saying their rosary with the beads held over the side of the bed, and others saying, 'Stop, stop, you dirty old dog,' and others yelling desperately to be jacked right up to their middies, and it often leading to nothing, and them getting up out of bed and riding a poor door knob and kissing the wooden face of the door and urging with foul language, then crying, wiping the knob, and it all adding up to nothing either." The hopelessness of the female condition, and Miss O'Brien's discontent with the first version of the book, leads in the revised second edition (Penguin, 1967) to Kate's decision to have herself sterilized as a final protest against the perfidy of men.

As Baba indicates, the realities of the female condition represent a complexity of eternal male-female differences, including undeniable factors of woman's physical condition, as well as the ideals and desires of both parties. Miss O'Brien said to Nell Dunn, "When I see a fairly handsome, middle-aged man of forty-five or forty-eight with a woman of forty-five or forty-eight, it is nearly always so, that the woman has spread a bit and the man is still quite attractive. This is biologically unfair and brutal. Fill in the scene by having a young girl go by in red jeans leaping up the steps and you know that that man wants to be with her and you know that he has every right to be . . . but what is terrible is that a woman has been brought up and is bred to believe that a man is hers for her whole life. It's unfair on the man as well as on the woman." Continuing the biological analysis, she added, "the reason I think on the whole that women are more discontent than men is not just that they get old sooner or that they have the vote, or that they haven't the vote, or that they bleed, but that there is, there must be, in every man and every woman the desire, the deep primeval desire to go back to the womb. Now physically and technically really, . . . a man partly and symbolically achieves this when he goes into a woman. He goes in and becomes sunken and lost in her. A woman never, ever approaches that kind of security.

A dramatic representation of this yearning is the beautiful and sad short story "The Mouth of the Cave," in which a woman, rejecting the sea route to the village, takes the cliff route and passes by a young girl just as the girl rises from the grass to pull on her clothes. The protagonist starts to turn in the opposite direction, instead returns, and watches the girl pass with head down. At home in her rented house, she asks the servant to set dinner for two outside and delays it until dusk; finally, dining alone, she relinquishes her obsession that the strange girl will certainly appear. But ever since she watches for the one face among passing school girls, and never again does she take the cliff route to the village although she desperately wants to. Since only a man can enter the woman's cave, the title symbolizes both the woman's physiology and the unfulfilled desire.

With no obvious intent to shock or scandalize, Miss O'Brien in these somber tones reveals the delicacy of the female condition. When penetration occurs, said Miss O'Brien to Nell Dunn, "To some extent [a woman is] being violated or invaded because when the maidenhead is first broken it is a rupture. Each time and for evermore she must carry the memory of that first rupture no matter how she desired it."

On the grave matters of pregnancy and the woman's sexual response, she admits that a man is still woman's enemy "much more than she is his enemy because he can abandon her and get on with his hunting but she cannot abandon him if she's impregnated. Also the physical make-up is so absurd. Technically it's haphazard. A woman can have orgasm from being touched by a man's tongue or his hand or his heel just as much as if she is penetrated by his penis . . . [But] a man's deepest need is to go into the woman's vagina, into the mother figure." Nevertheless it is a woman's sexuality that is the subject of Miss O'Brien's fiction; and, contrary to Sean McMahon's statement (*Eire-Ireland*, Spring, 1967) that "she has come to regard sex as a part of a normal life without any moral connections," the morality is clearly present in her protagonists' consideration for the love partner. In real life, she explained, "Morality is not the same thing as abstinence—I mean I say to my children 'Of course sleep with people if you want to but don't beget children.' That's my morality. That they shall not bring into the world someone who isn't wanted, by them, and who certainly isn't at the moment going to benefit from being alive" (Nell Dunn interview).

In fiction probably the most succinct statement of

morality—which is consideration—comes at the lyrically haunting conclusion of "The Love Object," the title story of the short story collection. In this story Martha is age thirty and has two children, ages eight and ten. The man, the "love object" is, once again, elderly, just as were Mr. Gentleman (*The Country Girls*) and Eugene Gaillard (*The Lonely Girl*). She is separated from her husband; her new love is married for the third time and has acquired fame and wealth and children. Martha rises through peaks of possessiveness to real love, only to find elements of dislike and hatred intruding, then the agony of loss and separation; and finally the relationship is restored to a condition of casual friendship. Martha learns that there can be no separation of identity from love, as she sought at the beginning: "He was in his way a serious man, and famous, though that is hardly of interest when one is telling about a love affair. Or is it?" As the relationship deteriorates into loneliness for her, Martha at one time contemplates suicide; but then her work with her sons, home ill from boarding school, restores some sense of being needed. In the end she learns to live with the hurt, and with continuing unfulfilled love for her lost lover; also she has developed the strength not to weep and the strength not to confide her real feelings to earn his pity. At the end, as they meet occasionally in cafés, she remembers, but does not utter a word about, "the man that dwells somewhere within me. He rises before my eyes—his praying hands, his tongue that liked to suck, his sly eyes, his smile, the veins on his cheeks, the calm voice speaking sense to me. I suppose you wonder why I torment myself like this with details of his presence but I need it, I cannot let go of him now, because if

I did, all our happiness and my subsequent pain—I cannot vouch for his—will all have been nothing, and nothing is a dreadful thing to hold on to."

Respect for the other person, as well as the staunch core of independence in the self, emerges in Miss O'Brien's fiction as a self-reliant preference for loneliness. She said to Nell Dunn, "I think that the price and premium I used to put on passion or on loving a man or of being in a state of love, was really, not trivial, because I was very intense about it, but was superficial, compared with the enormous seriousness and loneliness of the whole of one's life. And what I think is most important now is that I shall resolve to manage, that each person shall manage, to survive everything, and look out the window at whatever is their bit of sky and sink, not even sink into, but be glad of inanimate things, trees and sewerages, and advertisements, and cigarettes."

The year before *Girls* was published, Miss O'Brien's first play, *A Cheap Bunch of Nice Flowers* (1963), was published in *Plays of the Year*. Although she now calls this first attempt a "bad" play, reviewers' remarks on its performance in London also indicate the audience was not yet ready for the unpalatable feminine reality Miss O'Brien depicted. Yet the play—in which a feminist mother is dying of cancer while her unmarried daughter fantasizes a pregnancy by the mother's lover and to the end disbelieves in the mother's illness— embodies in reverse the fantasy that a young girl of Miss O'Brien's acquaintance invented, when Miss O'Brien was still a teenager. The "urbane" trend continues in the next novel, *August Is a Wicked Month* (1965), in which Ellen, divorced from her husband, sees him and their eight-year-old son Mark off on a camping trip in Scotland. Ellen, a continuation in some respects of the Caithleen character, is now age twenty-eight and has been divorced for two years. After a brief fling at an unsuccessful affair, she takes a vacation on the Riviera where, among wealthy film people, she learns that her son has been killed in an accident. The setting is described also in "Paradise," a short story about which she said, "once I had, so to speak, immersed myself in, suffered from, and emerged from that particular world of the rich and the bitchy and the heartless and also the terrible malcontents of the very rich, and the guilt that comes out—once I had exposed myself to that I didn't want to go to it any more."

The next novel, *Casualties of Peace* (1966), returns to the London setting with a heroine who attempts to heal the psychic scars left by a destroyed marriage. At twenty-six Willa McCord seems to live in a situation becoming more stable; her terrors derived from her past become proportionately less as her relationship with Auro, her dark lover, improves. But counterpointing her improvement is the damaged relationship of her household help, a married couple, Patsy and Tom. Tom's total disregard for Patsy's desires and complete satisfaction of his, and the earthy diction with which Patsy carries on her affair in letters and conversation, provide a contrast to the delicacy and fear of Willa. Again, Patsy's bluntness of speech and a dream she relates are drawn from life, for Edna O'Brien has said, "There is somebody who helps me in the house who tells me the most extraordinary things, half dream half awake, of how her husband's penis has fallen off and they're in the bath and she's trying to stick it back on but her hands are slippy with bath water and she is saying 'For God's sake stand still till I get it back on.' And she tells me this naturally without any probing on my part'' (Nell Dunn interview). Patsy's and Tom's disintegrating relationship shatters Willa's peace and makes her a "casualty of peace."

The next novel, *A Pagan Place* (1970) returned to the Irish setting but featured a marked departure in technique. Written in a second-person free-association style subtly modified to fit the demands of plot and chronology, *A Pagan Place* is reminiscent of the early passages of Joyce's *Portrait of the Artist as a Young Man*. To an interviewer of *Publishers Weekly*, Edna O'Brien said, "I wanted to make *A Pagan Place* a book that would seem to be a piece of life, yet have a mesmerizing quality to the language. I hope it reads like a little trip to a lucid hallucination." Here is the preadolescent Kate emerging into adolescence, being shocked into knowledge of sex, and finally determining to escape the home background by going anywhere. The first opportunity comes with a re-cruitment trip by two nuns who, ironically, stress the importance of the child's guidance by her parents in such a large decision. The child has by now acquired some of the guile necessary to the adult world and nods agree-ment, knowing she "would go away from them, far, far away, where no conveyance could bring them to [her]." Still there is nothing to assuage the guilt of departure, her mother's mournful howls ringing in her ears.

Zee & Co (1971) is the screenplay for the film *X, Y and Zee;* this most urbane of Miss O'Brien's published books to date continues Kate and Baba through the characters of Stella and Zee respectively. Stella, whose twin sons are age eleven, is more quiet and refined than

Zee; Zee is daring, devil-may-care, funny and witty, and most of all determined to keep her husband, Robert—an architect extension of Baba's husband Frank in *Girls in Their Married Bliss*. Part of Zee's strategy is sympathy and friendship for her enemy, Stella. The contention between the ego and alter-ego characters Kate and Baba is apparent in Zee's characterization of Stella: "There is nothing I hate more than soulful people, she's always a little out of breath, and she sees beauty in everything, specially in shit." In a passage of philosophy, Robert says, "Everyone has two types and one is true and one is false," to which Zee replies, "I often think people's letters are their true selves. Of course in the olden days people used to deliver them and wait for an answer under the casement." This talent Zee has for specifics, for exposing trite poses such as waiting under casements, evokes admiration. She proves a husband need not be lost to an affair if only the wife is resourceful and determined. Even Zee's name hints that she could be the last woman on earth.

The most recent novel, *Night*, completed in 1972, features the night time reveries of Mary Hooligan—a more mature, sensitive, and funnier woman than Zee. Removed to England and divorced, with a grown son now traveling in Europe, she remembers her childhood in the part of Ireland called the Barony of Coose, a "glorified bog" where "Purity prevailed, yet lapsed." Its people have "Not a baccalaureate among them, not even a martyr for the annals. Ignoramuses who couldn't tell cheese from soap, both being hard, off-white substances and tasting of curds when placed in the mouth." More than purity has lapsed where the beauty of hawthorns in May ("as if Coose were going to be the location for pageantry") and a noble tradition are mostly irrelevant: "Yet we are mentioned in the Norse books, in the *Kongs Skugo* and the *Speculum Regali*. We are not nonentities by no means." From a "botched" deflowering, Mary fled to England, the only "land across water" available. There Ireland returns to her thoughts when the themes of love and loneliness surface.

Night is a witchery of words that depends largely on the naturally rich, melodious, and archaic diction of Miss O'Brien's native County Clare. Yet the views of Mary Hooligan are those of a cosmopolite who, acknowledging her restricted Catholic background with pathos and humor, refuses to be confined in her thinking to any creed or nationality.

The importance of "society and the environment and the education that comes our way is so decisive in the forming of us," said Edna O'Brien. "I think of my own parents and think of their religious fanaticism . . . and . . . of . . . their various prejudices . . . . Had they grown up in another country, at a different time, a worse place, how different they would have been!" By contrast with the Irish, the English people are "courteous and distanced," but not "imaginatively exciting." She still finds the Irish people exciting, she said, but objects strongly that "they have a rather dreadful and historic habit of not brooking any other point of view or any contradiction; they don't like it. And that absolutely paralyzes me." Her insistence upon intellectual freedom perhaps best accounts for the candor of her works; the person she identifies with, she indicated, is the one capable of saying, "Yes you think that tree is oblong; you're allowed that privilege to think it but to me it seems to be a box."

The last three books, representing three distinct view-points, serve as corroboration of the extent to which Miss O'Brien lives this dictum of intellectual freedom. *A Pagan Place* features a rural Irish child confused by and confined to her home but determined to enlarge her horizons. *Zee & Co* offers the opposite extreme in the mature Zee's coarse, uninhibited thought and city-bred defiant action. Mary Hooligan of *Night,* fortyish and anticipating old age, has spurned an opportunity for wealth and something akin to the hectic social schedule Zee commands; Mary, extremely self-reliant, contrives ingeniously against loneliness but just as ingeniously preserves her precious independence.

2

Cinderella in Daylight, or Feminism and Shattered Shibboleths

That Miss O'Brien has been called a feminist develops not so much from an ideal or from a philosophical cause but from a realistic appraisal of the female condition and of the male-female relationship. Asked what the Cinderella motif means to her, as it appears in *August,* where Ellen wants a certain kind of man who would "control and bewitch" her, Edna O'Brien said, "I mean the metamorphosis from being outcast to being queen, to being accepted." Of the Prince Charming in this role, seven years after *August* was published, Miss O'Brien said, "As for the man who would bewitch her, I think I would use a stronger word now, the man who would possess her. I have a very strong pull and obviously conflicting pull towards god and the devil, and I used to anyhow, observe and be drawn towards men who seemed to me to have very strong elements of both, and who would exert power over one—over one's mind and over one's body."

Folklorists of the Cinderella motif explain that the mistreated, beautiful, and unhappy princess was an incarnation of Wisdom or Truth, the heavenly Sophia descended to earth. The devil principle in the popular version is the wicked stepmother or some force that retains her on earth and that is the embodiment of all earth's evils. In Miss O'Brien's hands the god who should mate with Cinderella and establish her in a new kingdom of happiness merges with the evil principle, so that, for example Dr Flaggler, a veritable Mephistopheles, chortles "You are not going to escape me, not now, not ever, you are not going out of my sight, you poor zealous wretch," and Mary calls her life with him an "Erebus." Mary's hope that "Dr Flaggler will mellow again" proves as vain as Cinderella's hope that her captors will see their evil ways and treat her well. Their insistence that Cinderella is inferior to the stepsisters paralles Dr Flaggler's attempt to destroy all self-confidence and independence: "you cannot make a life for yourself without me, it is beyond you, it is unattainable."

This archaic instinct in Miss O'Brien's work becomes a trenchant elucidation of the physical processes of maturation and age. As a result of self-development her characters realize that they must free themselves from the evil force, and generally they gather courage and walk away, as in the short story "How to Grow a Wisteria." When Nell Dunn inquired of her, "Can we protect ourselves from being left by men?" Miss O'Brien indicated with characteristic directness that "protection" is an inaccurate concept: "Well, this is the big big fallacy. Far from protecting—this is indoctrination again—I think far from protecting ourselves we ought to learn to believe and know that this [disruption of marriage] is going to happen. I don't mean that one should be bitter and say 'Oh he's going to leave me [next year]' but this is what blights friendships and marriage and everything—is this little Cinderella dream that you get one man and one woman and that it lasts, you know, they live happily ever after." Later, in commenting on the importance of the process of change, she reasserted that "the idea of marriage until 'death do us part' seems laughable, when one considers that the two people getting married have no idea what they are going to be like in their own minds, let alone what they are going to be like in relation to each other, in five years from the time they make that vow. I think that the most deeply forming relationships are in fact the most constant ones; they are constant ones that are changing within their constancy" (Durham interview).

In a sense Miss O'Brien's work may be viewed as a process of change from romance to realism—from the innocent view that an alignment with a male means happiness ever after to the stark realization that such is not possible. Actually, the popular Cinderella story is fraught with marital suicide in that Cinderella has lost the connection with abstract Wisdom or cultural benefits. In Edna O'Brien's work, Prince Charming is Eugene Gaillard, attracted to Caithleen Brady for her naïveté, but later finding her repulsive for the same quality.

Rather than representing Wisdom, which was originally a combination of Love and Knowledge, today's Cinderella must acquire Wisdom. Caithleen's first experience in this painful process occurs in *Country Girls* with Mr. Gentleman, an aged cavalier whose superb manners derive from his French origins, money, friends, and position, and whose attractiveness to women obviously develops from much experience. At their first meeting he wakes in Caithleen the unfamiliar sensations of sexual response: "There was a certain shyness about his smile, and as he shook my hand I had an odd sensation, as if someone were tickling my stomach from the inside." His appeal is partly to mother instincts; he projects the quality of masculine need, real or imagined. He becomes Caithleen's "new god, with a face carved out of pale marble and eyes that made me sad for every woman who hadn't known him." Like a Sir Galahad on wheels he appears twice at just the right moment, once to soothe Caithleen's nerves after a proposal from Jack Holland and once in Dublin after a tussle with a married man. Attentive and suave, he confines his caresses to kisses and carefully refrains from revealing any other physical objective until Caithleen is free to escape with him. Failing to appear for their vacation rendezvous, he sends a telegram explaining, "Threats from your father. My wife has another nervous breakdown. Must not see you."

Caithleen in *The Lonely Girl* is torn between a budding relationship with Eugene Gaillard and loyalty to her father who abducts her from Eugene. At home she quickly learns she can no longer seek help from either Mr. Gentleman or Mr. Brennan, who no longer love her. Her subsequent flight and return to the Gaillard residence in Wicklow immediately bring a deputation of her father, a cousin Andy, a one-armed man called the Ferret, and the "friend" who had helped her escape, Jack Holland. The provincials utter the usual expressions about the "poor innocent girl" and "only daughter," accuse Gaillard of having enticed her there under dope, and end in kicking him, as he lies defenseless on the floor, with their cow-dung-encrusted hobnailed boots, until the maid Anna blasts a hole in the ceiling with a shotgun and ushers all visitors out. The scene, ugly, nasty, and ludicrous, confirms Gaillard's low opinion of Irish rustics, including Caithleen, who knows "that he would never forget what had happened and that some of their conduct had rubbed off on to me." As their differences become increasingly apparent, Eugene asks the questions that have annoyed her: "How can you live two lives? In there [the Church] you're deep in it with Crucifixions and hell and bloody thorns. And here am I sitting on a wall, reading about atom bombs and you say 'Who am I?' For that matter, who are you and what are you doing in my life?" Knowing that Caithleen cannot be the idealized "simple uncomplicated girl" he had once thought her, Eugene nevertheless exhibits some aspects of Prince Charming through his efforts to improve her in health and appearance as well as in intellect;he gives her books and introduces her to his friends. Moreover, his greatest gift for enabling her to understand herself is teaching her to accept her body and his. But as circumstances increase the rift between them and she learns more about the physical relationship, she realizes "it is only with our bodies that we ever really forgive one another; the mind pretends to forgive, but it harbours and re-remembers in moments of blackness. And even in loving him, I remembered our difficulties, the separated, different worlds that each came from." Her summation of herself reveals her keen awareness of her inadequacies: "swayed or frightened by every wind, light-headed, mad in one eye (as he said), bred in (as he said, again) 'Stone Age ignorance and religious slavery.'" Such a severe self-analysis she concludes with an ironic comment on her religious situation and her inability to grope ahead: "Jesus meek and mild show me the right road."

The road becomes, through Baba's machinations, the road to England. The forced detachment from Eugene occurs finally because of Caithleen's jealousy of Gaillard's attention to anything but herself, of which he demands, "Am I to stop talking to people because you haven't learnt to speak yet?" She leaves him in a Dublin restaurant with a heart-breaking note calculated to bring him flying to her, continues to pursue him with phone calls and letters, and departs for England still searching the quay for some sight of him. The last chapter, an epilogue, comments on her job in a London store, her classes at London University at night, and the changing, more confident young woman who silently appreciates Eugene's introduction into his world, though it was "too soon." The possibility that the maturer Caithleen could have succeeded with Eugene is explored in "How to Grow a Wisteria," in which the heroine at last achieves for her own sake an imitation of the rural solitude she had formerly despised with her husband.

By the time of *Girls in Their Married Bliss* all opportunities for Eugene to live the role of Prince Charming, or for Caithleen to be transformed into his queen, have been shattered. The force that fixes her in his grasp is an unwanted pregnancy, while Eugene's small meannesses (such as paying the priest one Irish ten-shilling note instead of twenty pounds for marrying them), his authoritative exactnesses about small things, and his frequent tempers contrast with her guilt-ridden weaknesses and dislike of household duties. For a few hours' escape to a friend, Duncan, Kate reflects, "If only he'll give me this last chance, I'll change, reform, make myself so ugly that I will be out of the reach of temptation."

Kate's resolve falls short of accomplishment and Eugene condemns her "simpleton's servile ways" and lectures her, "The things you do, count, not your cheap little justifications." Although she is too humanly weak, he is not even human. Caithleen observes, "When people failed him he detached himself from them completely. They ceased to exist any more for him," so that her selfishness and furtiveness are countered by his of another kind, the only difference being his selfrighteousness. He searches for and finds her letters from Duncan and leaves a typed, incriminating note: "They are where you cannot find them, safe with my lawyer. I have no doubt but that they will come in useful." She looks into his ledger and finds an account of her evening, the lies she told to cover, the way her husband followed her, his comment on their marriage, "In a way it is a relief to know it is over. I always knew she would destroy it somehow." Baba's analysis of them is perceptive: "He was full of character of course and she wasn't. She wasn't bad, but like any woman she'd take mission money to buy clothes, or if she met some man she liked she'd pester him until she had loaded him down with the love bit. Knowing all this about her, he was so righteous he'd made a big splash about weeding his own garden. They were mad in two different ways." Countering her unconsummated "affair" with Duncan, Eugene has an affair with the maid, Maura, in his own house.

Outcast rather than queen, Kate then lives alone, seeing her son Cash mostly in parks and her husband at railroad stations. On one occasion she returns to the house with Cash's lost glove and observes the new "family" at dinner, Maura sitting in Kate's place at the table. A scene in the park is no less pathetic. Here, in the opposite of closeness to nature, she cannot sit on a swing with Cash because she is over sixteen. By contrast with the inhumane adult world, and almost in defiance of it, two children, one white and one black, enact "the birth of a baby on the slide. The coloured girl stood at the bottom and pushed a life-size doll up the slide and the little mother at the top slid down with the doll between her parted legs and the midwife took it from her. They had done it five times." Tessa, the colored girl, becomes a friend of Cash and tells him about her "good Mum" and her "real Mum." Kate hears her son say "I have another Mum too. She lives in my house with my father."The most pathetic—and climactic—scene revealing Kate's loneliness and nervous tension occurs when she follows a father and child to a ticket window and, in response to the father's inquiry, "Will we get a ticket for dolly too?" Kate pronounces an emphatic "Fuck." Thereupon she begins to talk to a voiced weighing machine and in frustration erupts into vitriolic abuse, smashing the glass. She awakes in a hospital. Later, after a night with a man, she concludes sleeping with someone is "A nothing, if nothing in the way of love preceded it." This is her "new-found knowledge." And from her unfortunate experiences and increasing Wisdom, she concludes of men "Some of course were flawed or hollow in there. Many, in fact." But with continuing inquiry into the mystery of life, she looks at an Englishman and speculates, "Was he?" The cost of seeking an answer is too great, however: "She would have to sleep with him to know. The only way of ever really knowing a man. The thought sickened her."

The Cinderella motif persists in *August,* although it is still in the process of being refined by experience. Ellen's interest in sex develops, after a year's abstinence, with Hugh Whistler, who comes to escape his mistress. He awakens her body to remembered pleasures, and Ellen tries not to be overpossessive; but his interest wanes and they stop seeing each other. Fleeing to the Riviera, she claims an open hunt on men but rejects several because "All her outings and hopes were veered toward being with a certain kind of man that controlled and bewitched her." The Cinderella motif demands this reaching for higher happiness with a selected person, and there is a halfway relationship with Sidney: "The minute she thought he wanted nothing she was able to flower, but if he reached out she closed and hardened." Among the movie colony is an actor, Bobby, who appears to be a man to aid her in reaching for the higher happiness. After the death of her son, Bobby is able to assure her that she will find a future after the desolation: "You've seen things—pretty things—come out of slums and slag heaps and manure heaps. You see those big indiscreet trees . . . . Something will come," he said.

With divorce in his past, all of Bobby's effort is directed toward the happiness of the present moment. "If I don't make you happy it's a waste of time," he says as he tries to teach Ellen to swim. But the differences always exist. In their one quarrel he calls her "goodie-goodie" and in their lovemaking later she is desperately enthusiastic: "Afterward she clung to him with her thighs, and extracting himself, it was as though it was he who was now the breaking rose and his strength had fallen away inside her like petals. 'Jesus,' he said." Her fierceness and his exhaustion account for his sudden departure and the end of this romance.

August marks a transition between the heroine's

earlier quest for self-development through marriage with a hero and the later knowledge that such is impossible. That dream was almost relinquished in *Girls* and was retained only in the ideal of a lover in *August*. Thereafter the Edna O'Brien heroine keeps the dream as a shadow of reality but alliance with a rare desirable male always, for some reason, proves impossible. The woman builds her future in direct strife with a male, as does Zee, or independently with an added burden of revenge for the damage caused by a man in the past.

Casualties of Peace is Edna O'Brien's most sensitive treatment of the extremely vulnerable woman who has talent and intelligence and offers love (including care of a nine-year-old boy) and yet is psychologically maimed by the villainy of a male. There are three men: the evil, sadistic Herod, ex-husband of Willa; selfish and violent Tom, husband of Willa's housemaid Patsy; and Willa's dark-skinned lover, Auro.

Willa's letters to Auro, written but never mailed, are found and opened after her death. These reveal the villainy of Herod who kept her incarcerated on a Swiss mountain while he likened her to a plant needing "a period of severe cold in order to encourage germination." He forced her to walk in terror at the edge of a cliff because he had been a tightrope walker; on four occasions only he carried her into his room where he tickled her into sexual frenzy and then withdrew with jeering laughter at the moment of need while he himself was impotent. He remarked, "Judge to what degree I love you" as he locked her in the cabin and explained her continued fearful stay as a need to be punished "because you are a woman." He said, "it's unfair that all monster things should be female" and staged a trial of her "deceit," in a ruin, and forced her to wear a black eye-shade while he exposed bits of her past. He returned her presents with a note, "Second-rate presents are for others perhaps, but not for me," and in a thousand little ways forced her to suffer in what she calls "slow poison" until she began walking at night to become accustomed to the dark forest and one night walked away.

Tom, a poor man's Herod, nearly dominates the book as he is revealed through Patsy's mind and conversation and through his own actions. The basis of the marital problem is that his sex is both a domination and an achievement for him, and he uses his wife's body merely to serve his own ends. Her relationship with Tom, shortly after the marriage, is "the pain from having had him so much and the other pain of wanting him, more." Indifferent to her feelings, he brags, "Great exhaustion tonight, supplying women," when he has supplied only himself. His work bossing a demolition crew, as well as his conversation, is violence-prone. He claims he can kill a man forty different ways, makes Willa's nose bleed while demonstrating a point in conversation, badly beats his wife even while making love to her. Patsy's letters to her lover turn his violent tendencies into actual violence, the mistaken killing of Willa.

Willa, who works in glass, prefers to believe that it reflects her own personality, "cold and chilling to the touch," while she tries consciously to become more vigilant and glacial to protect herself from more hurt. When she meets Auro, part Negro, he has compassion and an air of the exotic to attract her. Because of his inheritance he is vulnerable but because of his character and intelligence

                    Edna O'Brien

he is resilient. "Who smashed your nose in?" she asks and he replies, "I did. A man can't be perfect, it gets people's backs up." Her thoughts are permeated by Herod, however, and she remembers he said he had renamed himself to please his enemies; but Auro, not destructive like Herod, is defensive against misused love and for this reason admits, "When I'm relaxing my teeth are clenched." His persistence in working with Willa to seduce her into sexual pleasure is rewarded in a hotel for the aged, where, in spite of the atmosphere, he makes people laugh and delights Willa. From this trip she returns to her death; and Auro regrets that, without one more necessary year, he cannot convince her that love exists.

Neither a Willa nor a Patsy, Zee of *Zee & Co* refuses to be victimized by any secondary role. From the moment Stella and Zee's husband Robert are introduced at a party, Zee thrusts herself—all her wit plus her strategy of helplessness and dominance—between them to outwit them in the game of an affair. She arrives at Stella's dress shop to be fitted; she intrudes in a restaurant where they meet for lunch; she appears at home when they have planned a dinner for two and then goes to a restaurant with them—frustrating at the same time Stella's talent for cooking; she bribes a homosexual to gather information from Stella's shop assistant, Gavin, and learns their destination for a weekend so that she can interrupt with a phone call saying Robert's car has been stolen. When Robert attempts to sleep in the bathtub she waits outside the bathroom door and waylays him as he emerges; on another night after an apparently enjoyable time with Robert she attempts suicide. Saved by Robert, she yet becomes increasingly dramatic and desperate. She plans a strategic farewell party as Robert and Stella move into a new flat and thereby frustrates Stella's desire for a housewarming. At her party Zee dances wildly, gets Robert exceedingly drunk, then, after the others are gone, undresses him sufficiently for sexual gratification.

The next scenes were omitted in the film *X, Y and Zee* but bear intelligible relationship to the novel *Girls in Their Married Bliss*. Zee has found the keys to Stella's flat in Robert's pocket; and, in an interlude, a strange man (obviously Zee) arrives in Stella's apartment and carefully robs her. She meticulously chooses a ring Stella cherishes, just as in the early novels Baba covets Caithleen's rings that had belonged to Caithleen's mother. To this strange man, because with Zee's inventiveness he confides having been incarcerated in a psychiatric ward, Stella confesses psychiatric problems, as a continuation of Kate's experiences at the end of *Girls*. When Robert awakens the next morning Zee lies beside him with provoking evidences of having made love to him. Becoming angrier as they exchange words, Robert beats Zee viciously and methodically across the face with a slipper. Zee then arrives once more at Stella's apartment with her scars to testify to Robert's brutishness, and, knowing Stella is terrified of cats, brings a cat. Zee's final triumph is joint possession of Stella with Robert. The interchange of emotions that permits this relationship to develop is expressed in the final sentence of the play: "Zee's sigh of victory, Stella's of pent-up desire, Robert's of appeasement."

From this negative development of the Cinderella motif, shattering the shibboleth of woman's happiness as derived from man's love, Zee apparently reacts to

Baba's opinion of men and enacts Willa's revenge. Pauline Kael, in her review of the film, recognized that "love, knowing no honor, is treated not as a sloppy fact but as a triumphal statement—a battle cry in the war of the sexes." Praising the dialogue because "it sounds likely, because the wit belongs to the subject," she explains, "rich smart women who have never needed to develop their intelligence, who use their brains only to climb and to hang on to money and men, do become high-pitched and clever in this combative way. This honed edge of glitzy bitchery isn't an accomplishment, it's a dysfunctional weapon—the tic of wasted minds."

Having examined this type of life in Zee, Miss O'Brien makes her next character, Mary Hooligan of *Night,* more an intelligent earth mother than a bitch and a woman who deliberately rejects Zee's extravagant wastefulness. Mary's dominant quality is not so much sex as cerebration, though much of it is romantic recollection, through an entire night. Together Zee and Mary are far removed from the country girl living in fear of her father's drunken rages and of the Blessed Virgin's displeasure.

Whereas Zee's fierce determination to retain her husband asserts one aspect of female independence, that of refusal to accept dismissal, Mary Hooligan continues this dominant quality along with the other, loneliness. But with humor Mary regards the failures and inhibitions of her Irish background and removal to England; her losses and gains in employment, money, and housing; her earliest and latest inquisitiveness about living. She has lived through the birth and maturation of a son and the death of her mother, contends now with her father's lonely and vitriolic decline into inertia, and recalls her ex-husband's villainy. Through all this, she faces both independence and loneliness with integrity and fortitude. Having made "a written request to be buried on an island in the vicinage of Coose," she maintains, "I have no desire, not even in deathbed slobber, to be lumped in with other people and have them flustering around me and vice versa. Think of the tendernesses we would have to purport, the subsequent niceties, the clacking of tongues, handshakes, boneshakes, in order to live middlingly, peaceably, together for a long time, for ever maybe . . . . Do I mean it? Apparently not. I am still snooping around, on the lookout for pals, pen pals, cronies of any kind, provided they know their place, keep at distance, stay on the leash, leave me my soul's crust, and my winding dirging effluvias."*

The "soul's crust," that same core of being which Kate in *Girls* recognized, suffers its greatest damage and near loss in the disastrous marital relationship. In her long night of reverie Mary observes ironically that society has never provided places to accommodate the lonely souls who find no mates: "There ought to be crèches where poor people can go when their glands ignite, just as there are wailing walls, and temples to chant in." Dr Flaggler, to whom she was married, provided no human warmth. Of his attempt at lovemaking on the moors, Mary thinks "too much preparatory work went into it, it was a sad ballocks." When traveling to Europe with him, she remembers, "I would have embraced anything at the time, a sheaf or a pillar, and my hunger was such that my arms used to lollop out of their own accord, reach blindly for

*Permission to quote from *Night* has been granted by Weidenfeld and Nicolson, London.

some unfortunate person to hold on to." At first meeting he seemed "very aristocratic" and she admits having been "carried away with his airs and the interest he showed in me." Now she recognizes him as "one of the original princes of darkness." As an example of his humor she remembers a sign he placed in the lavatory, "having mounted and framed it, requesting that faeces only be put in the bowl." She muses, "The sign must have been meant for me as he didn't open his house or his gardens to any others, to the riffraff as he would say."

Among Mary's subsequent lovers, the best candidate for the Prince Charming role is the Duke. He speaks French, has money, influence, and friends; but Mary is too wise, "sincere," and independent to apologize for her preferences and her background. Being driven home by his chauffeur, she crouches to avoid being seen, explaining, "A Bentley is not my habitat, somehow I look better with a cart, drawing it by the thills." An elegant supper party, burdened with social pretense, has a frivolity and grotesqueness reminiscent of the aging Swann's summary of the Saint-Euverte party near the close of *Swann's Way*: "I watched their mouths, I watched their tongues, like tentacles, I watched their jaws, I could visualise my own. I had no business being there. The other lady at the table was sharp-bosomed and evenly tanned and she kept aiming her cleavage at the men like she was holding a motto to them." On the balcony Mary rejects the Duke's proposal for marriage: "I foresaw it all, the aubergine linen, the compost heap, the June, the July roses, Bridge nights, having to dress up, in gowns, in jodhpurs, in tweeds, the merry protocol. A whole new itinerary of lies and foils." Because she fails to sustain the Duke's fiction of bachelor availability, he takes her refusal as an insult; then she learns from a bystander that the Duke has "a wife in the country, a woman with a withered arm."

Whereas women have been traditionally the victims and also the villains in the battles of the sexes, Mary Hooligan can sometimes avoid being victim and always avoid being villain. In addition to her humor, her fierce pride and independence provide a shield for dignity; the wisdom born of experience enables her to foresee difficulties to which Kate would have fallen victim, and an inexhaustible ingenuity aids her to escape. One adventure briefly involves a man whose movements are surrounded with whirring machinery and timed by important connections that leave him only one hour for love. With his hands he literally manufactures an emission and questions Mary with businesslike courtesy, but he has no interest in or talent for possession. Mary departs, feeling, "There was a great boulder in my chest that I wanted to blast, to smash, to dislodge, to reduce to gravel or smithereens." Recalling Tom of *Casualties* who uses a woman only to secure his own gratification, this one-half relationship produces, out of Mary's need, one of her most triumphant non sequiturs: "I thought I would go home and masturbate, that that was what I would do, but it was early, it was so early, so early, so bright. The sales were on and there was fifty per cent off everything."

Since night is appropriate to thoughts of love, Mary recalls other men, in greater and more specific detail than does Joyce's Molly Bloom; and she exposes the crudities and contrivances of men. A trip to New York yields two contacts, one with a mogul who claims "when his wife had cancer of the brain, and his lady-love had cancer of the body, only then, filled as they were with tubes and physic, bound for death, only then could he fuck them at all." Mary quickly quells a suggestion that she go to his house: "All his family had ended up in incinerators. I baulked. I could feel a spot of cancer creeping into me like mist or verdigris and I am no one for being bed-ridden." The public inconveniences and her perception of imminent financial responsibilities attendant upon a proposal from a cab driver discourage another "romance": "I foresaw some joint, the signing of a book, a key, maybe two keys, a flight of stairs, sleaziness, a big bill and sub-sequent hassling." At home in London a waiter who attracts Mary because of his tight-trousered seductiveness discourages her, when he arrives at her home, with his long tales of a difficult life and his display of a grotesque black finger nail, "sprouting, elongating before my very eyes." She remembers, "First the nail repelled me, then the finger, then the hand, then the wrist, and gradually the repulsion spread and his farts filled the room, putrefied the atmosphere, brought on my customary choking."

The only men to sustain Mary throughout are the "guerillas," mere vestiges of godlike heroes: Moriarty, a stonemason; and McCann, the gunman whom Mary knows only by hearsay. Moriarty's friendship, a form of love never consummated, was abruptly terminated; and, because Mary guards the independence of others as much as her own, she thinks, "it probably got to be a bit of a noose around his neck." But given notice that she must vacate her rented premises immediately, it is Moriarty she thinks of going to.

Having nursed her mother through her last illness, Mary has presided over death; at the same time, befitting her namesake as ideal mother, she lives that role also, successfully and pleasurably, despite the additional burden of enabling a son to survive unwarped by Dr. Flaggler's imperious destruction. "The Lad," as Mary fondly calls her son, maintains his mental health largely because of a streak of his mother's rebellious and defiant humor. Mary recalls his childhood bout with "bowel problems," his scratching the paint off the lavatory seat and his punishment: "Dr Flaggler produced the water bag, and after insertion and later the movement, the lad was dispatched to his bedroom and locked in without benefit of bread or water. He says it is then he wished he had mastered the Chinese language, because it would have given him something to think about, as his mind was clamouring for new thoughts, theorems, puzzles." Her own intense and at times ribald cerebration enables her to project in an instant the mother aspect of woman as well as those of mate and survivor in terms of the mythological Triple Goddess who presides over birth, marriage, and death. An ordinary occasion, such as a proposed early morning visit of the window cleaner to her rented house, evokes an analysis of herself in this triple role, phrased as pure poetry: "I would be here in my bed, curled up foetus-wise between my hessian sheets, their hessian sheets, committing manslaughter in my dreams, or copulating with the succubi, being kissed by a whisker."

When Mary likens her confession of love to a fault such as "inheriting moles or an aquiline nose," the Cinderella dream has almost expired; and Mary's greatest love is for her absent son. The metamorphosis from outcast to queen is fully realized as the character Mary takes on the qualities of the Triple Goddess. Mary is an unquenchable spirit; a larger world of woman's being is at her command. Her mental autopsy on love, on youth, on vanished homesteads concludes with an invocation to the higher love: "Oh star of the morning, oh slippery path, oh guardian angel of mortals, givvus eyes, lend us a hand, lead us to the higher shores of life, of bolden, lawless, transubstantiating love."

3

Guilt by Inheritance

Mary Hooligan's savage irony, emerging through her tenderness, is no mere suppressed malice acquired during marriage to Dr. Flaggler. Ellen Sage of *August* has also a record of rejections of men although she schedules her vacation on the Riviera believing she longs "to be free and young and naked with all the men in the world making love to her, all at once." On the plane she sits by an attractive young man and speculates, "She could make love to him there and then, lie down and love this total stranger. She'd always wanted to. He had intelligent eyes. She was going to make overtures to every good-looking man she met. This trip was her jaunt into iniquity." But the greatest remaining portion of the book is a history of her conscious rejection of various men. On the beach she measures the competition and narrows the scope of her availability because here under the glaring sun "Only the perfection-people triumphed. The fat, the lame, the slobs, even the slightly blemished like Ellen would find it hard to pass as eligible. Unless of course she settled for people in her own category." She forces an amorous waiter to leave her room and rejects an American man who wants to treat her to dinner. Contrary to settling for

59

anyone, she withdraws from a rendezvous with the hotel violinist, fights off the room-service boy who attempts to rape her, and suggests hemlock to the actor's understudy whose humility she despises. Making love to the elderly Sidney, she fears she has failed him; later, fearing she will give a cab driver a venereal infection, she rejects his proposition. Finally, on her return, she rejects Hugh Whistler, whose lapsed love had motivated the departure.

The continence underlying these rejections she explains to herself as a process of selectivity aimed at finding the "certain kind of man"; however, her suffering is a form of masochism derived from guilt, religion, childhood memories, and her ex-husband's scorn. Her attitudes toward sex are haunted and distorted by knowledge of her mother's having been forced to submit to her father, though now, having been awakened to love by her ex-husband, she feels "her mother should not have been mean." Further, much of her present rejection of her religion was forced on her by the ex-husband who ridiculed her beliefs and practices; in spite of which, along with disillusionment about him, she lives in fear of the Church. Although she recalls she never left the priest's confessional feeling absolved, she has had her son secretly baptised. Moreover, these complex attitudes can be traced to "the great brainwash" begun in childhood: "Slipped in between the catechism advocating chastity for women was the secret message that a man and a man's body was the true and absolute propitiation." Burdened by these contradictory admonitions, she feels guilty about occasionally having wished for some reprieve from care of the child and fears she has never loved anyone totally unselfishly. She tells Hugh Whistler, "I want to love someone other than myself," and only intense discontent with the self can explain her desire "To cease to be me."

Like Stephen in Joyce's *Portrait*, her concern with herself is that of a seeking, developing personality: "Nothing moved or spoke to her from the real world now unless she saw in it an echo of her own castaway plight." After the death of her son and the loss of the actor Bobby, the chimera of indifference replaces narcissism. Yet the core of being that Kate recognized, or Mary Hooligan's "soul's crust," exists in Ellen also; she describes her heart "like a nutmeg. Some of it had been grated by life but the very center never really surrendered to anyone"; and with this center intact Ellen survives these tragedies to face a cooler autumn.

Edna O'Brien traces mixed emotions of guilt and rebellion to childhood, especially in the novel *A Pagan Place*. When that common fortification against fear, whistling in the dark, occurs to the child, she curtails the effort because, "Only men should whistle. The Blessed Virgin blushed when women whistled and likewise when women crossed their legs." But when religious rules mean enviable piety, the mother's defiance of the Church for a friend places a strain on the daughter too: "Your mother was very straightforward and committed a terrible sin once, went to a Protestant service, to Manny Parker's mother's funeral. . . . But even after the forgiveness came the priest made a show of her by giving a sermon about it and although he didn't mention her by name everyone knew and she got up in the middle of the sermon and walked out, tapping her umbrella on the tiles as she went." The father, returning from the monastery

     Edna O'Brien

where he had been "taking the cure," is refused a ride home by the Protestant minister because the point of origin for his journey represented the opposing faith. The child remembers when her sister fainted in the confessional and, as the door burst open, thudded onto the floor of the church; the incident was attributed by the locals to too much buffing of her fingernails, but the knowing child calls it fright.

Fixed in the places, as well as the conditions of childhood, the "you" of the story seeks escape from these but also, and primarily, from her family. Descended from the land-owning Irish but shiftless, disastrously attached to thoroughbred horses, and given to drinking bouts, the father strikes fear into mother and daughter. Horses and drink keep the women in a turmoil of apprehension, but when the bout is over and remorse sets in, the brink of disaster still is ever near. Against the ever-rising tide of family debts, another field can be sold, while the mother's flock of foul-dropping hens preserves the family's meager respectability.

Respectability, enforced by religion and education and family pride, urges the developing child toward intellectual and spiritual awareness but paradoxically not toward fulfillment. The home is equipped with a flush toilet that functions only erratically, and the father prefers to urinate in nightly ritual from the top step at the back door. (Ambie, the hired man, uses a can, which he empties out his bedroom window.) The parents' grunting activities behind a closed door and the mother's tickling game with the doctor, as well as teasing of the child by such local persons as the white man named Nigger who does "pooly" in the town pump, incline the child toward an unvoiced awareness of the physical body. At the same time the consciousness of ancient knowledge outside the Catholic faith and outside the school textbooks impinge upon the child's insularity.

Some of these elements date from before Christianity. The fort of dark trees near the child's home is "a pagan place and circular. Druids had their rites there long before your mother and father or his mother and father or anyone you'd ever heard tell of. But Mr. Wattle said that was not all, said he had seen a lady ungirdled there one night on his way home from physicking the donkey." A witch woman who cured the child's father of eczema cackles to herself as she gathers plants and stones. In a nearby field the owner of a local pub found an ancient collar of gold; the "torcs," as they were called, were identified with early Celtic heroes and deities, and the finding of one made him famous. Many local ruins are reported to be haunted so that the child blesses herself in passing them, while a black dog is permitted to disturb a wake because "A black dog and the devil were one and the same." An example of the irrelevance of religion to practice, or the contrast between paganism and Catholicism, occurs when the father, after having beaten the daughter savagely for an escapade with the local priest, buys special "Pentecost water to sprinkle on a yearling." As if hearkening far back to the Cattle Raid that made Cuchulain famous, "Her lineage was in a studbook and he worshipped her." It remains for Mary Hanrahan to contrast the realities of the present with the glories of the past; nevertheless, in *A Pagan Place*, the father's only unassailable virtue—bravery against the Black and Tans—can be traced to an Irish quality of fierce stubborn pride. To prevent the Black and Tans from commandeering his ancestral home, he burned it to the ground; the present family cottage stands near the old cellar hole. The mother's brother had organized "ambushes against the Tans."

When the father's favorite daughter, Emma, returns from Dublin at the age of seventeen, unmarried and five months pregnant, the household is plunged into righteous consternation; and, by reading Emily's diary, the mother acquires an education in pornography. From this society's barbaric treatment of the unwed mother, after the birth of the child, the girl flees into the freedom of a dignified type of promiscuity in Dublin. Refusing a visit from her own mother, and choosing abandonment as a way of life, the girl burns her mother's pitiful letter in the candle flame of a night club without so much as a glance at it.

The loss of one daughter does nothing to enlighten the parents about their attitude toward the second daughter but only stiffens them in their love for respectability. The climactic incident of the book is the passage of the young girl from childhood into womanhood. With the violence of the father in the background, the scene becomes a common pagan initiation ritual; exhibiting the archaic instinct once more, its pattern is that of Jesse Weston's *From Ritual to Romance,* complete with the girl's mysterious illness, seduction after crossing water on a houseboat, beating, and survival as a new person.

The experience is preceded by a terrified flight from a cousin who exposed his chest and by unexplained maladies such as sleep walking and vague discomforts that a chest Xray cannot confirm. When a popular young priest arrives, the parents desire a share in the prestige of entertaining him. At their house he writes a frankly seductive verse in the girl's autograph book:

> My body is but a cabbage
> The leaves I give to others
> But the heart I give
> To you.

On an outing with the family he announces he and the girl will visit Hilda, a wealthy local woman, and then he abandons Hilda to take the girl on a houseboat. There, the seduction almost accomplished, she freezes into fear while he masturbates. At home she finds that the outraged Hilda has spread the news throughout the town. When her father furiously and rhythmically beats her, she experiences in masochism the sexual triumph that the priest had only begun: "Each onslaught was a surprise because he got more impassioned as he went on. The flap between your legs began to heise up and down and you encouraged that and the pleasure that you forsook when you expelled the priest's finger began again, and the tumult that should have been his to witness took place unbeknownst to him on that rattly bed while other parts of you smarted and cried." Hitherto a nervous, frightened child, afraid of entering many rooms in her own house, the child is remarkably different after the beating: "You were not afraid to be alone in that room. That was how you knew something had changed."

The change is not only physical but also mental, particularly in the attitude toward the parents. Formerly the mother and daughter had collaborated in self-defense against the father's shiftlessness and drunken violence. In this incident the mother offers no protection, and, apparently for the first time in years, agrees with the father's course of action. Amid sharp pains after the beating, the daughter's awareness is simply phrased: "There was tea being made. They were talking amicably. They were collaborators."

Subsequent conscientious mortification of the flesh does little to exclude from the mind the new knowledge of sex and exhibits how much enslaved are both mind and body to this great mystery. In an approach to the ill Nigger's shack with an offering of food, the girl overhears this lonely man talking with an imagined woman; even the flutter of leaves simulates the sexual rhythm, "their wide green palms opening then tightening, letting in and keeping out the light." But of the relationship with the parents, she knows, "there was a breach for evermore."

Various childish rhymes of escape and far-away countries encourage the longing to be free of home and childhood; a song of departure ("Now is the hour") heard in Dublin, the tropical places the seductive priest spoke of, coincide with the far places described by a recruiting nun who visits the local school, where her talk, ironically, emphasizes the number of pagans in the world and the necessity of bringing pagans to the happiness Christ intended for them. In the girl's decision to become a nun, the recruiter stresses the importance of guidance by parents. There is no pretense of a "calling" but, knowing the importance of guile, the child nods agreement.

Edna O'Brien has called herself "only a guiltridden

Irish woman."Yet, while submission to "inherited ground-less fears" accounts for many of Caithleen Brady's inadequacies, and development must be away from these, she has as best friend an alter-ego named Baba who points the way for her. Although Caithleen dominates the first two novels, Baba speaks in chapters 1, 6, 7, and 10 of *Girls* and gradually develops into the dominant character in Zee and Mary Hooligan. When asked if there was an original for the character of Baba, Edna O'Brien answered, "I think I did have school friends who were the opposite of myself, and they were extrovert and mischievous, more mischievous. I was drawn towards them as I always am towards opposites. But now I think that it was partly my other person, my alter-ego. I had a sort of streak of submersed rebellion in me always, which I never let out, unfortunately; I was really too frightened, too meek. And I don't think that the meek should inherit the earth, really, because then I don't think agriculture or productivity of any kind will get done." The cruel, yet healthy, jeering of schoolmates may be observed in *A Pagan Place;* its extension in the character of Baba is her practice of scornful psychological reduction of the timid and clinging Caithleen.

Caithleen in *The Country Girls* has ample opportunity to measure her meekness and inadequacies against others and to develop under Baba Brennan's influence when her mother dies. With the father away on a drunken binge, the mother has gone, ostensibly, to visit relatives. Caithleen is thrilled to accompany the Brennans for an evening at the town hall with its varied program of tap dancing, banjo playing, singing, clowning, and raffling, followed by an intermission and a performance of *East*

Lynne. The dusty curtain that will not rise, the poor
makeup of an actor, the shuffling, noisy audience barely
visible in a crowded room lit only by smoky oil lamps
are naïvely observed by Caithleen. When the girls are
asked to sing at intermission, Baba uses the opportunity
to humiliate Caithleen (who only pretends to sing) by
stopping in the midst of the song: "And there I was,"
relates Caithleen, "seen by everyone in the hall with my
mouth wide-open as if I had lockjaw." The news of the
mother's death, brought during the play, shows the
friends in stark new light, with guilty consciences. Baba's
only expression of sympathy is, "I'm sorry about the
bloody aul' song." Jack Holland takes Caithleen aside and
whispers, "So help me God, I couldn't do it" and confesses he refused a loan to Caithleen's mother. The
father, singing in a pub, manages to pass out dramatically
at hearing the news. Mr. Gentleman acts with characteristic restraint but fails to invite Caithleen to stay at his
house. At home the two greyhounds moan upstairs and
Mr. Brennan emerges as the strong, sympathetic friend,
the father Caithleen should have had. Molly, the Brennan
servant, provides unexpected care and sympathy.

After three years at the convent school, Baba and
Caithleen contrive a dismissal for writing a dirty poem
partially read out by a nun, and thereby prove that
religious limitations may serve useful purposes. The ar-
rival at home after dismissal becomes a scene in which Mr.
Brennan must defend Caithleen against her father, and
Mr. Brennan recognizes that Caithleen has always been
"Baba's tool."

In *The Lonely Girl* Eugene Gaillard offers Caithleen
one way to develop independently of Baba; but Caith-

leen's aunt has always claimed that divorce (Eugene's chief fault) is worse than murder, and when Caithleen is returned home by her father, the school children taunt her as she passes through the village. Her former friend, the seemingly enlightened Mr. Brennan, can only say "I'm very disappointed with you," and his wife, who had sat in pubs drinking gin with strange men, now has "got religion" and calls her "mad, to think of a man like that." Mr. Gentleman likewise has turned religious and, obviously ashamed of the times he and Caithleen had kissed and said "I love you," he now calls her a "very foolish little girl."

Detained at her home, she protests to the visiting priest when her father is once more dangerously drunk, "It's as big a sin for my father to be like that as for a man to have two wives." The priest replies, "I'm surprised at you, to speak of your good father like that. Every man takes a drink. It's the climate." To solve her "problem," he gives her a book, *The Imitation of Christ,* and recites the Act of Perfect Contrition. As he goes out the door, he assures the aunt, "She'll be all right now."

Escaped to Eugene once more, she remembers his jeering "Only egomaniacs see Christ as God come especially to save *them.* Christ is the emanation of goodness from all men," and she realizes her changed attitude when she goes to Mass and finds "the people distracted me—their coughing, their ill-fitting clothes, and that sour smell which comes from drying their faces with dirty towels." But when the aunt sends a pious letter claiming she and the father cannot sleep for worrying about Caithleen in the hands of that evil man, she realizes how emotionally, if not intellectually, she is still bound to her people. She believes it "cruel" not to set the aunt's mind at ease by a reply; and, later, when the father and the Bishop arrive, she feels guilty about turning them away.

When in *Girls* Caithleen is unhappily married to Eugene, who shuns her "as if she were a deformed person," she seeks some recreation away from him but phrases her guilt still in the terms of the Church. Delicate about physical things in spite of having been reared on a farm (in *The Lonely Girl* she became ill, she remembers, when Baba told her about breast-feeding), she vows to "expiate all her sins by sinking into domesticity. She would . . . scrape marrow from the bone and mix it with savoury Marmite to put on bread; she would put her lily hand down into sewerages and save him the trouble of lifting up the ooze, and hairs, and grey slime that resulted from their daily lives."

By contrast with guilty and inadequate Kate, Baba is crass, openly greedy for money, and, removed from pious morals, able to characterize herself and others with profound insight: "I had a brazen, goodlooking face and was afraid of none of them, not even afraid whether people liked me or not, which is what most people are afraid of, anyhow." She is married to a builder, Frank, who is even more vulgar than she, and thinks his money can buy him status. He has his secretary send ninety-four telegrams to the wedding, with workmen's names on them because, claims Baba, "He'd die if he didn't get a bigger number of telegrams than anyone else, or make the wittiest speech." Her mother favors Frank because he has money, while Baba calls herself the "bloody, sacrificial lamb" in her wedding party. Far from becoming a victim of anyone, however, she induces Frank to support her unborn child who is not his.

In addition to Kate's own staunch independence, two forces, then—the scorn of the ex-husband whose love is perverted into hatred, and the opposing example of the conscience-free Baba—function to lead Kate (and her namesakes) away from parochialism.

How deeply sexual fears are ingrained, Edna O'Brien revealed in the interview with Nell Dunn when she said, "I don't think I have any pleasure in any part of my body, because my first and initial body thoughts were blackened by the fear of sin." The intellect, however, defies these emotions, and Miss O'Brien said, "I believe in only one or two sins, cruelty, killing, and injustice. These are sins; everything else, lust, sex, adultery, covetousness are venial, you know, they're just little flaws." Yet Miss O'Brien also admitted, "I was married once and after four or five years I then became very attracted to somebody else and the only reason I didn't sleep with that somebody was my permanent and pervading guilt. I couldn't come home to my husband, who was then my husband, and look him in the eye and make tea, I couldn't. And this wasn't niceness or anything, it was deep-rooted fear, he might kill me or something if he found out" (Nell Dunn interview). Guilt in itself is a type of fear, derived from excessive consciousness of fault; and a fear of having an "incontinent heart," in the personal odyssey conveyed by these novels, combines with the fear of retribution from the "wronged" party. As a result, when the development of the Kate personality proceeds to *Casualties,* Willa's terrors of anything physical have been transferred from religion to Herod. "Obviously I am rooted in the idea of Original Sin," Miss O'Brien said recently. Asked what the term means to her, she replied, "It means that one has been marked, if not completely destroyed, by the blemishes of will and flesh. That's what it means to me."

If communication, and hence self-expiation, of these fears cannot be achieved with a sophisticated husband there is even less possibility the fears may be conveyed to an uncomprehending family. In the story "Cords," Claire is age twenty-eight; from her visiting mother's viewpoint, "she'd lost her faith, and she mixed with queer people and wrote poems. If it was stories one could detect the sin in them, but these poems made no sense at all and therefore seemed more wicked." The mother, who lives on a chicken farm and arrives carrying a suitcase secured with binding twine, clashes with her daughter's friends—a man with his wife and his mistress. The country ways cannot be shed, nor does she desire to adopt the sinfulness of these city people. A piece of mascara she calls a tealeaf on her daughter's eyelid; Green Park across from Buckingham Palace she pronounces "Very good grazing." The mother's severest indictment of the daughter's friends, "They're not sincere," is countered with Claire's exasperated, "And who is?" The mother's insistence that she was a good mother brings from Claire a story of childhood horror and revulsion when her mother had callously told her about the doctor's incision of her toe; the mother still fails to understand why this detail is a failure of motherhood. For Claire, "Since her mother's arrival every detail of her childhood kept dogging her"; the mother returns home early, laden with packages purchased at Claire's expense, but with this generation gap painfully widened.

Babas, although they bruise many egos, remain the best assurance for Kates to develop; and Miss O'Brien makes the strife between them an open battle in *Zee & Co.* The psychological bruising that results from the clash of ego with alter-ego explains why Robert's affair with Stella arouses Zee's cunning will to fight as none of his previous affairs had. The remaining step in self-perfection, after the confident Baba is transformed into ruthless Zee and defeats Stella-Kate, is the creation of a fully integrated personality. This is the achievement of Mary Hooligan in *Night*, where the country past impinges on the city present, and religion, the ex-husband, and the near friend converge through dramatic rumination.

In the Nell Dunn interview Edna O'Brien said that she thinks the loss of memory would be the only holiday in the world, yet Mary experiences an entire night of memory; and her greatest achievement is not loss but the maturity to regain laughter and to disdain faults and failures. The Irish typically, said Miss O'Brien, "make noise about history and use it as a resting post on which to lament"; therefore Mary confides, "I was ever one for eventide. I have so many maudlin memories of it, the soft feel of wallflowers, or is it heliotrope, showers of rain, smoke curling up, the dogs famished, mavourneen, the pig badgers and the dog badgers out, warring, evening auguring towards night, and such a momentum of tears, and for what, and for whom—Lil, Boss, Dr. Flaggler, Tutsie." These four people, constituting Mary's mother, father, husband, and son, stand out from the remnants of the Irish country past which are, metaphorically, the paws that "come out from underneath the well of the bed, all vying for a handshake, some gloved, some ungloved." The four persons stand out also from the present environment among people who "cling to me like sloths. How they weigh, how they prey upon me. I am prepared to vouchsafe that they are attached to my scalp by means of brooches, so tenacious are they."

Among paws and people, the friend Madge is recalled near the end of the night and of the novel, and Mary admits, "things are thinning out, handshakes getting more limp, birthdays getting forgotten." Crude and essentially unlikable, Madge is not the ego of Kate but an extension into dislike of the alter-ego Baba and therefore a dismissal of the need for such a confidante. Mary reflects, "A big wall or a gangrene has risen up between us. We can't forgive. Or rather we can't comprehend the spite that possessed us. I won't see her again, not till her funeral probably." The last visit to Madge began with Madge's abusive greeting, "Sonofabitch," proceeded to a quarrel, and ended with an unenthusiastic reconciliation, upon which the "farewell carried with it the nugget of all the others and the waves we exchanged were artifice itself."

The clinging of memories becomes the dominant theme of this novel; so much so, in fact, that Mary Hanrahan, musing about her prenatal existence, remembers "I wrote and asked if she [Lil] had any inkling, any hunch, about the exact colour of her innards, my earliest known abode." Mary accounts in detail for the rationale of this letter, inviting the mother to "sally into inventiveness"; then she is struck with another memory: "No sooner had I posted the letter than I realised what a débâcle I had made.

My mother is dead. To make matters worse, my mother is only fairly recently dead and I realised that the postman, who is a dunce and a dunderhead, and bunioned from his peregrinations, would deliver it out of habit." From her father's reaction to this brazen "untowardness," she is, fortunately, saved by the expanse of water between England and Ireland.

Mary recalls nursing her mother through a long, haggard illness, the memories which crowded upon the mother's flickering mind, her dreadful death fantasies. During these, "some children went by, a butcher's son, a veterinary surgeon's son, a druggist's son, children all connected with the dark themes of life." Too close to death himself was the canon who came to shrive her: "Once he came with the chalice empty. After that the curate came. Poor canons, old, grey, teetering, lonely and loony, with their frock coats and their faithful housekeepers, that breed of dark warted women that do wait upon them." The funeral, "a comic event," scarcely justified these sober preparations; the mourners were "Grievously stung by nettles," distracted by passers-by, and treated to the "ludicrous disaster" of Mary's fling into grief, which resulted in a sprained ankle. Memories are not improved with the father's resentment of his daughter's waywardness in her subsequent escape, once more, to England. At the close of the novel she remembers her last visit to him, a Christmas duty, his truculence surpassed only by that of Marty, a cousin they visit. At Marty's home, an extension of her own father's lonely condition, the salt is prodded from the cellar with a rusted safety pin, a litter of pups shelters in his sister's "grey fur

     Edna O'Brien

tippet" on the kitchen floor, the wardrobe contains dishes
and hanging flannel trousers, and a rash on his hand
spreads from nervousness occasioned by their arrival.

But Mary has recognized that she must go beyond
the "terrible tempest" to the "real pageant," and the
ultimate guilt is not religious but the pain of others'
expectations of her and the necessity she feels to chart
her own way. For this reason she calls herself "a mur-
deress of three—Boss, Lil, and Lightfoot [Flaggler]." She
exempts the other important person, the lad, who "more
than likely has the irons over me" through his own guilt.
The memories of the lad are told partly through his
notes and letters from childhood to maturity; and her
love for him, in which his independence and her loneliness
are partly resolved, no doubt explains the novel's
epigraph, "She is far from the land/Where her young
hero sleeps."

4

From Copybooks to Finnegans Wake

"When I was young," Edna O'Brien said in an interview for *Hibernia* (December 3, 1971), "I always wanted to be a writer and since then I have realised this dream. It's some sort of ache or dissatisfaction which makes me go on. It's something terribly intangible—almost like seeing something superb in the sky, in behaviour, or in the land, and seeing it is not enough. You have to somehow set it down for someone else to see, even though that sounds arrogant." What she sees, as her vision becomes apparent through her fiction, has remained consistent in regard to her commitments to Ireland, to the theme of love, and to writing as a dedication.

The style during these years has developed from the simple and barren naïveté of the young Caithleen with her revealing touches of ingenuousness ("I felt badly about being the cause of sending them solicitors' letters but Eugene said that it had to be") to the discursive ruminations of Mary Hooligan who reels off exhaustive lists like those of Samuel Beckett's *Watt* and converses with herself in a stream-of-consciousness-with-plot technique somewhat like that of Molly Bloom. Most of the fiction

77

is written in the first person, which enhances both its verisimilitude and, one suspects, the critical tendency to treat it as autobiography. The best passages of the early novels are those scenes which reveal contrasting personalities—in *The Lonely Girl,* when Gaillard comes to tea with Joanna, when the deputation of virtuous godfearing farmers call upon the agnostic Gaillard to retrieve Caithleen's honor, when the locals in the pub insult Gaillard and Caithleen—and these point to a successful career in drama. *Girls in Their Married Bliss,* the most discomforting of the novels, is blunt and direct in diction. The same attitudes on love, or the female condition, or religious friction may be phrased more subtly in the later works. The progression in style has permitted experimentation in technique, notably in *A Pagan Place,* which is written in the second person with the child-heroine identified only as "you," the father as "he," and the mother as "she." The two kinds of fiction—the Irish and the urbane—are produced from two life styles in Ireland and in England. Caithleen from County Clare is, in Baba's terms, a "right looking eejit" (a Clare expression), and a heroine may appear "streelish" in Ireland and "wanton" in England. The last novel, *Night,* marks a maturity not only in style and content but also in perception about the home land. Using real Irish names, Miss O'Brien has now created a territory as Faulkner did with Yoknapatawpha, and she projects for her future work, outside the Barony of Coose with its residents' characteristic confusion of soap and cheese, an area beyond Coose proper called Bohatch, where "they don't distinguish between a slash hook and a table knife. Beyond that is Derrygoolen," she said, and it is inhabited by persons "who know nothing about cheese, soap, farm utensils, or cutlery. That's a kind of dead end!"

This mergence of Irish geography with artistic vision develops naturally from Miss O'Brien's concern with memory. The technique of *A Pagan Place* and of *Night* is the use of memory through contrasting personalities; but the similarity between the "you," who makes a "mind and soul trip" into childhood, and the mature Mary Hooligan is the Irish background. "It's amazing," said Miss O'Brien, "childhood really occupies at most twelve years of our early life (that was in our childhood; I believe now they escape from home at age seven), and the bulk of the rest of our lives is shadowed or colored by that time." Acknowledging Proust as the "great architect of memory," Miss O'Brien describes herself as a person "afflicted and blessed with the obsession of memory." Her family, she said, "are here, they're in my throat . . . and I suppose I'm haunting them as much as they're haunting me."

Admitting that "Maybe one can make more of a choice than people like me are prone to do," on another occasion (for *Hibernia*) she said, "I think every good writer is a good masochist! possibly because the only revenge is on the page. They are masochists and victims in life and all masochists are just sadists waiting to be cured." Writing requires, also, a conscious exclusion of distractions that distort the original perception. "I often wish now that when I had written my first book that I had kept it and had written ten more before getting published," Miss O'Brien said. "Because although one thinks one is very free and private, you don't really know what you are doing, and are affected afterwards by what you are told" (*Hibernia*). This purity is necessary because, as Miss O'Brien said at Durham, "what makes a novel, or any work of art, valid, is the degree of truth and authenticity behind it." Of the great writers—Chekhov, Tolstoy, Strindberg, Pirandello—she said, "their soul is what gleams across the page. And the characters, and the language they use, the story they tell, is really only an index of what is pouring out of their souls. I don't mean their ego, I mean their spirit, their divinity." She cites Tolstoy, Chekhov, and James Joyce as the major writers who influence her; and among these, the influences of Joyce are most obvious. "I think without question nobody has made the progression with language that James Joyce has done. Nobody has gone as far as he did with both *Ulysses* and *Finnegans Wake*. He was the most pure man to have worked at that pitch, to have driven himself almost beyond his own ability" (Durham).

In the short story collection, three stories—"The Rug," "An Outing," and "Irish Revel"—evoke the atmosphere of Joyce's *Dubliners*. "An Outing" is a picture of paralysis in which pride interferes, and the people are trapped in their pathetic situation. Mrs. Farley, age forty-six, works as a housekeeper and connives to buy a sofa to impress a married friend who brings a spark of romance into her life; but upon the day of delivery, the only day her husband is away, after months of planning she decides its drabness precludes her having the friend visit her home. Instead they spend the day walking the streets and she realizes too late that he would have understood. In "The Rug" the mother searches several months for the identity of a benefactor who had sent a beautiful gift of a black sheepskin rug, and then learns it had been delivered by mistake. She stoically accepts her disappointment as she surrenders the prize. Her sense of loss derives only partly from relinquishing the rug and largely from "her own foolishness in thinking that someone had wanted to do her a kindness at last."

"Irish Revel," the best story in the collection, offers a West of Ireland version of Joyce's classic, "The Dead," although, as the title indicates, the living here are mostly concerned with living. Mary bicycles from her mountainy farm home, thrilled at an invitation, only to find she and three other girls have been "invited to lend a pleasant and decorative atmosphere to the party, and of course, to help." Like Lily of "The Dead" who is at the outset "literally run off her feet" and kept running most of the night, Mary cleans and serves and dodges the lecherous clutches of the drunken O'Toole. At home, Mary reflects as she works, "at least it was clean dirt attending to calves and pigs and the like." Throughout, Mary yearns toward the absent face of an English painter who had visited two summers before and had sent a drawing of Mary which was used at home to sweep dust onto. For her the distant music is her memory of dancing with the painter "to no music at all, just their hearts beating, and the sound of happiness."

Having worked most of the night and slept in one bed with three other girls—with the bedroom door barricaded against O'Toole—Mary rises at dawn to find that O'Toole in unrequited lust has retaliated by turning the taps on five porter barrels and flooding the stone floor of the bar. Outside, when Mrs. Rodgers bails the porter, it washes away the night's frost and reveals the cow dung once more.

Unlike the snow of Joyce's story that finally brings to

Gabriel a consciousness of universality, the frost has come like the descent of winter on Mary's heart. During the party her orange drink had been laced with gin and her Confirmation pledge broken; the total experience of the party teaches her, through weariness and disappointment, to relinquish her dream of the English painter. Yet she walks her bicycle with its flattened tires home to the small white-washed house, in her naïveté still believing that the burden of living she carries in her heart can be lifted by someone who will love her. Her living death is confinement to that house, a "little white box at the end of the world." Nor can the frost be romanticized into a pure common good: "The poor birds could get no food as the ground was frozen hard. Frost was general all over Ireland; frost like a weird blossom on the branches, on the river-bank from which Long John Salmon leaped in his great, hairy nakedness, on the ploughs left out all winter; frost on the stony fields, on all the slime and ugliness of the world."

The influence of Joyce, and especially of "The Dead," was noted by Fritz Senn ("Reverberations," *James Joyce Quarterly*, Spring, 1966) in *The Country Girls*. Also the style of *A Pagan Place* echoes the early pages of Joyce's *Portrait*; for example, the child's confusion about words produces an analogy between glacé cherries and people's eyes, "when they were upset or when they had fever." Each chapter begins with a child's bit of rhyme or doggerel about people or things in their proper places, but soon the images of escape from those places culminate in the child's sudden announcement that she has a vocation because the promised cloister is in Belgium and religion offers at present the only means to fly by the nets. *Night* features a rural stripling, "a fellow with unmatching eyes," who recalls the blind stripling of *Ulysses*; and Mary's "winding effluvias" evokes a flickering gleam of Anna Livia Plurabelle. *Night's* greatest resemblance to Joyce is in its indebtedness to the soliloquy of Molly Bloom with the particular Edna O'Brien touch of attachment to the Irish past. Just as Molly remembers Algeciras, Mary recalls the Irish countryside: "The low farm houses were so right, so friendly, so safe and even then I said to myself what am I missing, and why do stone walls and white gates and sheepdogs and blond roofs speak so, along with little bushes and the clotheslines and the garments going swirl swirl and all the other inconspicuous things and the white birds, the gulls, and the black birds, the crows, and the black-and-the-white birds, the magpies."

The evolution of Edna O'Brien as a writer, however, bears as its closest resemblance to James Joyce her regard for authenticity; indeed, believing letters reveal the true self, she read his letters and paid tribute to him in a beautiful and moving biographical essay, "Dear Mr. Joyce" (*Audience,* July-August, 1971). In her fiction her authenticity reflects the same scorn for pretense that Joyce experienced when he read Seamus O'Kelly's stories and wrote in a letter to his brother (November 20, 1906), "The stories I have read were about beautiful, pure faithful Connacht girls and lithe, broad-shouldered open-faced young Connacht men, and I read them without blinking, patiently trying to see whether the writer was trying to express something he had understood. . . . Maybe, begod, people like that are found by the stream of Killmeen only none of them has ever come under my observation, as the deceased gent in Norway remarked."

Yet, if Edna O'Brien has learned from Joyce, in particular in the rich prose of Mary Hooligan, she remains her own woman. More than ten extremely productive years of writing have yielded two fundamental attitudes that are important to Edna O'Brien and that reveal her artistic development. She recalls an early lesson in writing from a letter in which Chekhov admonished Gorki on the quality of grace, which is "making the most movement with the least effort." Miss O'Brien believes writing should give this impression and therefore in the early novels tried to "pare it down." For this reason she said, "I'm also more interested in the boughs and branches and twigs of trees than in the foliage. Foliage is very nice, but I like sentences to be spare." But she indicated, also, a progression to the style of *Night*: "I like the words to be rich—each individual word—but not too many of them. I do set myself a task, or I'm beginning to—that one should be able to read any line or paragraph of a book—out of context even, and find it to be start-lingly good, even with not knowing the story." The second artistic objective has to do with content. Miss O'Brien said, "I think artists have a duty—I may not have always observed it, but as I get older I'm at least coming to admit it—and their duty is to make life better—a little bit better— for the other people who are living it, and for themselves." Part of the second resolve may be realized through an example of the first, in the journey-of-life motif from *Night*: "And still the journey is not without its come hithers, not without challenge, not without incentive. . . . The very flowers of the field get inside my head and the blossom that hangs from the hedges and I talk to them, to the herds, to the humans, and heady on to the thought of the warm inn and the wheaten bread and maybe an ascen-sion."

Selected Bibliography

I. Primary

Nonfiction

"Dear Mr. Joyce." *Audience* 1 (July–August, 1971): 75–77.

Novels

August Is a Wicked Month. New York: Simon and Schuster, 1965; London: Jonathan Cape, 1965.

Casualties of Peace. London: Jonathan Cape, 1966; New York: Simon and Schuster, 1967.

The Country Girls. London: Hutchinson, 1960.

Girls in Their Married Bliss. London: Jonathan Cape, 1964; New York: Simon and Schuster, 1968.

Girl with Green Eyes. London: Penguin Books, 1964 [a reprint of *The Lonely Girl*].

The Lonely Girl. London: Jonathan Cape, 1962; New York: Random House, 1962.

Night. London: Weidenfeld and Nicholson, 1972.

A Pagan Place. New York: Alfred A. Knopf, 1970.

Plays

A Cheap Bunch of Nice Flowers, performed at New Arts Theatre, London, premiere November 20, 1962. Published in *Plays of the Year,* vol. 26, edited by J. C. Trewin. New York: Frederick Ungar, 1963.

"Last Rites for a Young Marriage," *Vogue* 158 (July, 1971):
  92–93 [an excerpt from *Zee & Co*].
A Pagan Place, premiere November 2, 1972, at Royal Court
  Theatre, London.
"Wedding Dress; a Play for Television." *Mademoiselle* 58
  (November, 1963): 134–45.
Zee & Co. London: Weidenfeld and Nicolson, 1971.

Screenplays

Girl with Green Eyes, adapted from the novel *The Lonely
  Girl*, directed by Desmond Davis with executive producer
  Tony Richardson; a Woodfall production, released by
  Lopert Pictures, starring Rita Tushingham and Peter Finch,
  1964.
Three into Two Won't Go, adapted from the novel by Andrea
  Newman; directed by Peter Hall with producer Julian
  Blaustein for Universal Picutres, starring Rod Steiger and
  Claire Bloom, 1968.
Time Lost and Time Remembered, written with Desmond
  Davis from the short story "A Woman at the Seaside," by
  Edna O'Brien with original title "I Was Happy Here";
  directed by Desmond Davis with producer Roy Millichip
  for Rank Organization; released by Continental, starring
  Sarah Miles, 1966.
X, Y and Zee, produced at Shepperton Studios, London,
  starring Elizabeth Taylor, Michael Caine, and Susannah
  York, from the screenplay *Zee & Co*, released by Columbia,
  1971.

Short Fiction

"Come Into the Drawing Room, Doris." *New Yorker* 38
  (6 October 1962): 47–55. Also in *Winter's Tales*, vol. 8.
  London: Macmillan, 1962, pp. 143–76. Also in *The Love
  Object* under title "Irish Revel."
"Cords." *The Love Object*, London: Jonathan Cape, 1968;
  New York: Alfred A. Knopf, 1969, pp. 131–48. Also in

The Sphere Book of Modern Irish Short Stories, edited by David Marcus. London: Sphere, 1972.

"Good Friday." *Spectator* 200 (25 April 1968): 522.

"How to Grow a Wisteria." *The Love Object,* pp. 91–99.

"Irish Revel." *The Love Object,* pp. 101–30.

"Let the Rest of the World Go By." *Ladies Home Journal* 82 (July, 1965): 48–49. Also in *The Love Object* under title "How to Grow a Wisteria," revised.

"Lovely to Look at, Delightful to Hold." *New Yorker* 40 (28 March 1964): 38–44. Also in *The Love Object* under title "An Outing."

"The Love Object," *New Yorker* 43 (13 May 1957): 42–52. Also in *The Love Object,* pp. 11–46.

"The Lovers," *New Yorker* 38 (16 February 1963): 28–34.

"The Mouth of the Cave." *The Love Object,* pp. 83–89.

"My First Love." *Ladies Home Journal* 82 (June 1965): 60–61.

"An Outing." *The Love Object,* pp. 47–69.

"Paradise." *The Love Object,* pp. 149–89.

"The Rug." *New Yorker* 39 (16 March 1963): 55–57. Also in *The Love Object,* pp. 71–82.

"Sister Imelda." *Winter's Tales,* vol. 9, edited by A. D. Maclean. London: Macmillan: New York: St. Martin's Press, 1963, pp. 170–92.

"Which of Those Two Ladies Is He Married to?" *New Yorker* 40 (25 April 1964): 49–54. Also in *The Love Object* under title "Cords."

"Woman at the Seaside," *Mademoiselle* 60 (March 1965): 168–69. Also in screenplay *Time Lost and Time Remembered.*

Short Story Collection

The Love Object. London: Jonathan Cape, 1968; New York: Alfred A. Knopf, 1969.

II. SECONDARY

Bannon, Barbara. "Authors and Editors." *Publishers Weekly* 197 (25 May 1970): 21–22.

Dunn, Nell, ed. "Edna." *Talking to Women*. London: Macgibbon and Kee, 1965, pp. 69–107.

Kiely, Benedict. "The Whores on the Half-Doors." *Conor Cruise O'Brien Introduces Ireland*, edited by Owen Dudley Edwards. New York: McGraw-Hill, 1969, pp. 148–61.

McMahon, Sean. "A Sex by Themselves: an Interim Report on the Novels of Edna O'Brien." *Eire-Ireland* 2, No. 1: 79–87.